# SCOTT JOPLIN
## ARRANGED BY LAWRENCE ROSEN

T0034035

## 18 RAGS
### IN EASIER VERSIONS

ED 4099

ISBN 978-0-7935-4621-3

## G. SCHIRMER, Inc.

DISTRIBUTED BY

HAL•LEONARD®
CORPORATION

7777 W. BLUEMOUND RD. P.O. BOX 13819 MILWAUKEE, WI 53213

# CONTENTS

Maple Leaf Rag ............................................................. 2

The Easy Winners ......................................................... 6

Swipesy ...................................................................... 11

Ragtime Dance ............................................................ 15

The Nonpareil ............................................................. 19

Paragon Rag ............................................................... 23

Elite Syncopations ....................................................... 28

The Entertainer ........................................................... 34

Weeping Willow .......................................................... 40

Palm Leaf Rag ............................................................. 44

The Chrysanthemum ................................................... 48

The Favorite ............................................................... 54

The Sycamore ............................................................. 58

Heliotrope Bouquet ..................................................... 62

Lily Queen .................................................................. 66

Pine Apple Rag ............................................................ 70

Kismet Rag ................................................................. 74

Magnetic Rag .............................................................. 80

# FOREWORD

About a hundred years ago, the piano style known as "ragtime" started a revolution in American music. The name that comes first to mind whenever ragtime is mentioned is, of course, Scott Joplin. The publication of his *Maple Leaf Rag* in 1899 in Sedalia, Missouri was probably one of the key events in the history of popular music. This was not Joplin's first published rag, but it was the first big hit to come off the presses of John Stark and Son. For Joplin this marked the beginning of a remarkable partnership with Stark that continued for several years and resulted in the wonderful series of piano pieces collected here.

We've all heard the *Maple Leaf* and *Easy Winners* and *The Entertainer*, and many of us have heard other Joplin rags as well, and maybe we've tried to play them. Sometimes they're not so easy to play. So, while preparing our new edition of Joplin's complete rags for piano (Volume 2020 in the Schirmer Library of Musical Classics), Lawrence Rosen and the editors at G. Schirmer decided to work on another project that might prove just as valuable: a volume of slightly "easier" versions of some of the best pieces. The result is what you see here, a selection of 18 rags that we hope will bring hours of musical satisfaction for the pianist who might not yet have the polished technique or the patience to tackle the originals.

Arranging Joplin's pieces this way is not always a simple task. The challenge is to make the playing easier while preserving the music. Lawrence Rosen has done a splendid job, adjusting an octave here or a chord there without compromising the melodic or harmonic integrity of Joplin's work. We're confident that you'll appreciate the ease and fluency of these versions, and perhaps the experience will lead you to explore the originals as well. Enjoy!

# MAPLE LEAF RAG

Scott Joplin
1899

**Tempo di marcia**

**Trio**

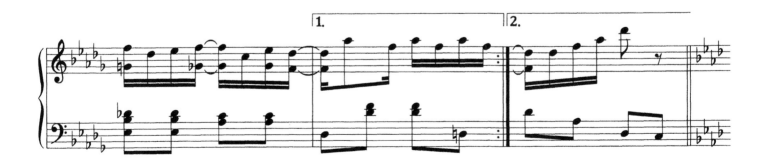

*Fine*

# THE EASY WINNERS
## A Ragtime Two-step

1901

**Introduction**
**Not fast**

*Fine*

# SWIPESY
## Cakewalk

Scott Joplin
and
Arthur Marshall
1900

**Slow**

*Fine*

# RAGTIME DANCE
## A Stop-time Two-step

1906

**Not too fast**

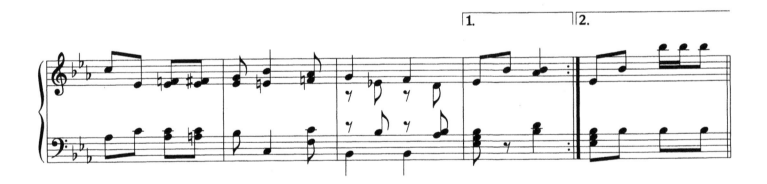

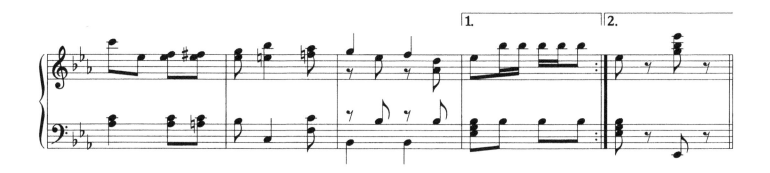

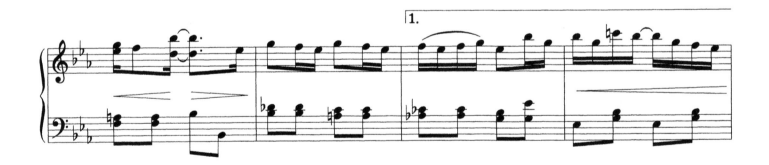

*Fine*

*Respectfully dedicated to Miss Mildred Ponder*

# THE NONPAREIL
## A Rag & Two-step

1907

Notice! Don't play this piece fast. It
is never right to play "ragtime" fast.
—Author

**Slow march tempo**

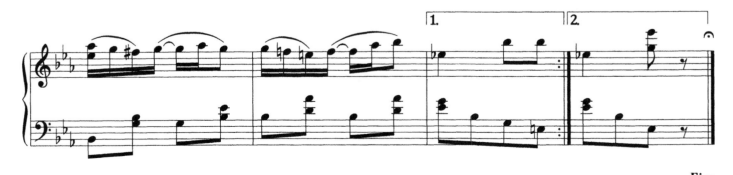

*Fine*

*Respectfully dedicated to the C.V.B.A.*

# PARAGON RAG

1909

Notice! Don't play this piece fast. It is never right to play "ragtime" fast.
—Author

**Slow march time**

**Trio**

*Fine*

# ELITE SYNCOPATIONS

**Introduction**
**Not fast**

1902

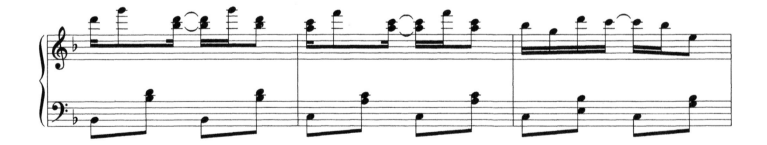

*Fine*

*Dedicated to James Brown and his Mandolin Club*

# THE ENTERTAINER

**Introduction**
**Not fast**

1902

*Fine*

# WEEPING WILLOW
## A Ragtime Two-step

1903

**Not fast**

*Fine*

# PALM LEAF RAG

1903

**Play a little slow**

*Fine*

# THE CHRYSANTHEMUM
## An African-American Intermezzo

**Introduction**
**Slow march tempo**

1904

50

*Fine*

# THE FAVORITE
## A Ragtime Two-step

**Introduction**
**Slow march tempo**

1904

*Fine*

# THE SYCAMORE
## A Concert Rag

1904

**Tempo di marcia**

*Fine*

# HELIOTROPE BOUQUET
## A Slow Drag Two-step

Scott Joplin
and
Louis Chauvin
1907

Notice! Don't play this piece fast. It
is never right to play "ragtime" fast.
—Authors

**Slow march tempo**

*Fine*

# LILY QUEEN
## A Ragtime Two-step

Scott Joplin
and
Arthur Marshall
1907

**Notice!** Don't play this piece fast. It
is never right to play "ragtime" fast.
—Authors

**Moderato**

*Fine*

*Respectfully dedicated to the Five Musical Spillers*

# PINE APPLE RAG

Notice! Don't play this piece fast. It is never right to play "ragtime" fast.
—Author

1908

**Slow march tempo** ♩ = 100

*Fine*

# KISMET RAG

Scott Joplin
and
Scott Hayden
1913

**Introduction**
**Not fast**

*Fine*

# MAGNETIC RAG

1914

**Allegretto ma non troppo**

**Tempo l'istesso**

*Fine*